W0254329

COSMOPHILIA

TALONBOOKS

COSMOPHILIA

RAHAT KURD

POEMS

Talonbooks
278 East First Avenue, Vancouver, British Columbia, Canada V5T 1A6
www.talonbooks.com

First printing: 2015

Typeset in Arno by Typesmith
Printed and bound in Canada on 100% post-consumer recycled paper

Interior and cover design by Typesmith
Cover photograph "There Be a Storm a Brewin'," 2009, by Flickr User: Bradley Gordon (Creative Commons 2.0)

Talonbooks acknowledges the financial support of the Canada Council for the Arts, the Government of Canada through the Canada Book Fund, and the Province of British Columbia through the British Columbia Arts Council and the Book Publishing Tax Credit.

LIBRARY AND ARCHIVES CANADA CATALOGUING IN PUBLICATION

Kurd, Rahat, author
Cosmophilia : poems / Rahat Kurd.

ISBN 978-0-88922-946-4 (PAPERBACK)
I. Title.

PS8621.U73C68 2015 C811'.6 C2015-904123-6

CONTENTS

The beautiful, almost without any effort of our own, acquaints us with the mental event of conviction, and so pleasurable a mental state is this that ever afterwards one is willing to labor, struggle, wrestle with the world to locate enduring sources of conviction – to locate what is true.

– ELAINE SCARRY
On Beauty and Being Just

In Kashmir the real thing is what we are after.

– SUDHA KOUL
The Tiger Ladies

SHISH MAHAL

I am the mirror palace of the annihilated.

In the arc of my splendour the shattered shelter –

In the vault that houses the lamp every glittering facet is mine.

Every facet a crystal of pain, formed in every heart that yields to me –

And every heart that yields its pain to me reflects mine.

BURNABY, EVENING, APRIL

the stranger passed here,
to let the stranger pass there.
– MAHMOUD DARWISH

I walk through shards of glitter today.
Through a glass and steel house of teenage desire –

expensively curated, easily bruised.
Then cars stream past, all threats and cold shoulders.

Asphalt and concrete mock my every step: Absence
sufficed you before. Is this poetry, the frail thread

that pulls you here now? Private lawns inhale their poisons.
Against the slant of gold light, compassion moves

its hobbled instrument. Spring evening on a downward slope
to your stunned absence, written in the faces of the women

to whom you splendidly belonged. Endurance,
written there too, forces back my disbelief; my glance,

faltering, to the floor. I walk today
not in the beginning of loneliness

but in dread of its return, as if the black coat
I'd slipped off and forgotten years ago

were to appear on that park bench, folded, waiting,
unmistakably mine. Someone knew I would pass this way,

stranger descending a wide bowl of earth ringed with mountains.
Their blue when dusk swells and blurs them

recalls blue domes of Shiraz, hills of besieged Sarajevo,
held breath of Srinagar at curfew, its mothers fearful;

its teenagers impatient to begin
the beautiful arguments we will never begin.

Our footprints won't keep pace in any other dust.
We won't trace our names on the walls of old Delhi,

we won't warm our hands on the walls of old Kashan.
Except for the May night I read Faiz in Shahid's English

and you delighted everyone with Faiz in his own Urdu,
we spent all the time we would ever have

describing borders of suspicion we'd circled in tedium,
hands up, passports high, on this unceded ground

I now profane with every step
I take in your absence.

Gold light grows fainter,
each rebuke more insistent, plainer:

Who would welcome you, after Burnaby?
What language, broken, avails you now?

In memory of Usamah Ansari, 1985–2008

COSMOPHILIA

It was hereditary for an embroiderer's son
to be an embroiderer's son.
— FRANÇOIS BERNIER
Travels of the Mughal Empire, 1663

1

We will never meet.
I will not live
to know her name.

I will sew my initials
into the fresh length of wool
she will inherit
when worn and faded.

In my smallest stitches
she will discern
with pleasure
the shine of silk filament.

Across half a century
our fingers will touch,
here, on the bright border,
when she reads
in the spacing of each leaf
curling backward off a vine,
the rhythm of my breath,
the blood-beat in my deft hand,
a collaboration
that insists and insists,
in the midst of snags,
tears, and ordinary despair,
on being looked at.

In circles and half-circles,
in tight arabesques or loose spirals
my lines expand out, almost double back;
as if in restless, rigorous thought
each complex elaboration
integral to the harmony of the whole;
not rushing any part of the particular,
not the curled tip of the smallest leaf.

Petal by petal, paisley by paisley,
I make summer creep and flourish
across a wintry field
to wrap her shoulders
in a single enduring embrace.

2

At nine, still slipping
shyly to the edge,
still learning how to look,

she will become fluent
in the flowers and birds
of her cuffs and collars;

love a certain chain stitch
worked in diamonds
of moss and camel suede.

When sixth-grade boys
raid the cloakroom,
lift the fringed, fur-lined vest
high above her reach, laughing,
Did you kill it yourself?

She will decide
to keep it plain,
plain as possible.

She will make it work.

3

From the ubiquity
of the machine-made
she will fatigue,
turn back, look again;
follow the lines of my thought
even to the Naghsh-e-Jahan;
trace elaborate tile patterns
inside the jewel of Lotfollah;
envy Istanbul merchants
for knowing by the flick of a thumb
the softest grades of antelope hair;

go suddenly shy
with the carpet seller in the Pasar Seni;
as if, on the wooden floor piled high
with familiar woollen mats and cushions,
the mere exchange of Kashmiri greetings
set off the sound of army truck tires
spitting gravel and contempt, boots on the ground
of their separately known Srinagars;
sudden snowfalls of memory
chilling two strangers in the Malaysian jungle.

4

I have no apprentice
and will leave no heir.

It's true I refused to hurry,
to let threats and flattery
jostle me from reverie,
force my stitches
along crude lines in fear.

No matter how devoutly
my patterns and fabrics
sing *Kashmir, Kashmir,*

still the army will tear up the forests
transform our cool riverine valley
into the long sludge of resignation.

Let them say my needle and thread
were powerless to save sons and brothers;

if it brings them solace,
let their too-young ghosts accuse mine
of a lifetime shackled to useless ornament.
I loved apple-blossom drifts on royal lawns,
I loved chinar leaves swirling on blue water.

Those who tied thread
at Chrar-e-Sharif
to give substance
to their softest hope

now reach for stone
to convey their agony;

for iron to measure
the ruthless erasure
of our gentle daily rhythms.

Over the slashing
of our finely woven world
she will be too anguished
to write a word; too angry
having flown so soon
this frayed latticework,
our fragile bowl of habitation
houses burned, hillsides stripped,
muddied, roiled by flood.

5

I will remind her
how to pick up the thread
when the end of mourning comes;

how to mark the rhythms that mark us
as we cross our given spans of time.

We must search quickly, quickly
for the tools that best fit our hands:

Even at our vanishing point, the marks we make
must stun with delight, the force of life itself.
Death must be satisfied with just our bones.

6

To prepare for the work
on cold mornings,
she will press
the same stiffness
I press from my finger joints
wrapping both hands
around ritually prepared
cups of hot liquid
lowering chilled faces
to the rising steam.

I will have become her creation
as much as she is now mine –

Across five decades we will *adaab*
in mutual admiration at the skill
– oh my rival, whose was the greater?
with which we made each other up
– the arts by which we kept ourselves alive.

GHAZAL: IN THE PERSIAN

What secrets – and from me! – you kept in the Persian!
Rules beg to be broken as I grow adept in the Persian.

That love Faiz refused to give again, Lal Ded refused from the first.
Her fierce solitude sparks panic in every soul, except in the Persian.

Must it always be war when we meet? The times we meet are so graceful –
Your elegant farewells never falter, never ask me to return in the Persian.

I lost Urdu as I lost Kashmir, every time I left my beloved women.
I found a circuitous way back to them, uphill, by stealth, in the Persian.

They ask me, after such bitter loss, what possible consolation?
I tell them dry-eyed in the English: I know how Khusro wept in the Persian.

The spy blunders most where he hoped to impress.
Licensed to kill it in Arabic! The joke's inept in the Persian.

The warmongers jeer: "Even the Taliban write poetry!"
But my improvised device pulls Sunni closer to Shia in the Persian –

Listen: Shujaat Husain Khan weaves Mevlana in the sitar strings of Hind;
Kayhan Kalhor bows his kamancheh's deep approval, in the Persian.

As a serene heart? Rahat's *that* comfortable in the Persian.
As paradox? Being Rahat's *kheili mushkel* in the Persian.

GHAZAL: ON EID

Aunt Sabiha's splendid ritual? Urdu verses lavished by email. Tempered black on Eid,
Sabera memes the occasion, hits Reply All: *omg mom why are u smoking crack on Eid*?

Sultan Ahmet's minarets poised for liftoff; unrivalled Lotfollah's creamy pink dome –
Rent a gym, spread a sheet: instant mosques I look back on, when I look back on Eid.

Each year you complain: Hijra, lunatic, mocks solar clockwise in widdershins skips
But your delight shines all twelve months when your birthday falls smack on Eid.

Black velvet backdrops a neon Kaaba. Heavy attar of roses antiques Grandfather's gun.
Kashmir wails on vinyl. Bring the imam! We love it loud at Dad's den of slack on Eid.

Cold thicks our plot: a marriage dismantled, as Ramadan mantles seven summers *karim*.
Speak the blessing: so hollows our fiction! Does a heart or the facade now crack on Eid?

Modest eyes, silent mouths, I'm hungry of ear. My ears crave a female muezzin to praise.
Yalla, *ustaza*, sing the Takbir! Please God, just once, not some tuneless male hack on Eid.

Broken threads, friendless cities, whole scarred mountain ranges – Rahat's lost legions.
Why ask for their names? She embraces their ghosts when her arms hang slack on Eid.

NASTALIQ CONFESSES AT TWILIGHT

An evening telegram brings the news
that Nastaliq is dying.

I find Naskh
pacing the hall outside her room
in tight shoe leather;

Nastaliq *adaabs,* all watery sheen
of old silks, all rumpled elegance;
rasps – *how kind of you* –
from her deathbed.

"Quit calling it that!" Naskh complains,
"You are not dying!
I've got Thuluth on the line
and Knotted Kufic wants to come see you –"

He turns to mutter into his phone.

Nastaliq raises an eyebrow,
and glances at the door –
when the creaks of his footfalls resume,
she closes her eyes in contempt.

"Knotted Kufic! What can she possibly say to me?
We don't even work in the same language –"

She motions to me for cigarettes –
as she strikes her match I snap on the key light,
take my place behind the ancient camera.

"And anyway, look at her!
All that controlled perfectionism,
the impossible complexity of all her knots,
and still Andalusia slipped right through them –

She could have learned
from my open, dancing agility,
you know. My lightness of being –

Iqbal's Masjid-e-Qurtaba
etched into my lines – not hers –"

She assures me, streaming smoke,
coughing, that she doesn't mind the glare –
she likes the whir of the motor –

"But tell me why you are here.
What do I mean to you?
What is this cinema for which
you wish to record my confessions?"

I tell her the moving image comes closest
to her fragility and her quickness; like hers,
its visual language leaps ahead
of our attempt to catch its sense –

I tell her how anticipation of pleasure
warms the body as it moves down the aisle
towards a seat in the darkened theatre.

"It might please you
to be remembered this way –

She looks at me sharply.

"It will please you, I think,
to be able to cling to my lines
as if you have never dreamed
in any other language.

What is it
I have allowed you to forget?"

In that instant we become as women
between whom there have never been secrets.

"Yes," I say, "there was such a cinema.
I used to walk there with someone I loved."

She nods, and waits. Then she says,

"You would have loved anyone
who walked with you along such streets,
to such an end. And now?"

"I no longer have any reason
to walk down that street.
The cinema was torn down;
I don't know if I ever loved anyone;
if I was deceived even by the feeling.
And talking of it now –"

"Is to talk of what is dead,"
she says firmly. "You are no Ghalib
lamenting Delhi streets and markets
the vengeful British razed after rebellion;
no Zinat Mahal dreaming of lost jewels
from her prison in Rangoon. You
must not become one of the haunted."

I abandon script
and say how stranded I feel
in the dashed-off tangle of her lines;
that some part of her meaning
nearly always escapes me.

She laughs and coughs, delighted.

"I wanted to run before I walked –
to fly before I ran.

You know I appeared as a bird
in a dream to the calligrapher Mir Ali
in fourteenth-century Tabriz?

He awoke thinking of how the eyes
lift the sense of the words off the page –

He awoke with an idea of writing
that moved in the shape of wings.

I exulted to think readers would pursue me;
to think they found me worthy of pursuit –

I loved turning back
to see plainly written in their faces –
even the best calligraphers and poets –
the fear that I might elude them –"

I tell her impulsively I wish
she could have outrun entirely
the ones who used her worst,
bending her lines
into blunt instruments
for the erasure of other scripts –

She listens, and for a moment,
covers her face with her hands –

"Generals and bureaucrats,
those tyrants –
don't remind me –"

Then she faces the lens,
resolute again.

"Perhaps I began to die
after what the soldiers did
to the women of Dhaka –
I still have nightmares –

After such crimes,
perhaps it is right that I should die –
the twentieth century
was full of such humiliations –

But you must remember,
over all the centuries before,
how I drew them to me –
the learned and the playful,
Turk, Safavid, and Brahmin,"
she recalls dreamily,

"It mattered only
that I gave them a way
to be together –"

It's true my origins are imperial,
but I am the result of strangers
overcoming their mistrust
to draw nearer together;

In my turn, it was right
that I should bring to me
those who wanted most
to know each other's voices,
recite each other's verses –

With me, the poets were inspired
to go farther – with me they dared –"

Another glance towards the door,
and she beckons me closer –

"They dared to boast of loving God
better than the guardians of religion –
risking the charge of blasphemy
for the sake of being generous –"

Now her eyes close again,
her head rests back against the pillows,
breathing out another plume of smoke.

"But who will be left to lift the sense,
to write and recite with my wings?

Will they be turned over to Naskh,
clicked into zeros and ones?

I won't be so easily translated –

I was not made
for people to sit alone at night
ruining their eyes
in search of lost expression.

You know I lived in the breath,
in the quick movement
of human hands. What else
can satisfy the human heart?"

WAGAH BORDER

I do not know
Why yet I live to say 'This thing's to do;'
Sith I have cause and will and strength and means
To do't. Examples gross as earth exhort me . . .
– SHAKESPEARE
Hamlet

1948

How shall I come,
with great arrogance
or dust on my head,
to Wagah border?

What wouldn't I risk
for the Sindh of it
and the Hind of it?

Here I am.
Whose army
dares to meet me?

For my wrath,
whose soldiers
will scramble
to clear the way?

Who will watch me
grimace at the cattle prod
of national identity;
dig in my heels
at the forced march
to the meanest point of entry;
shrilly proclaim myself
peace T-shirt
to their full-dress parade;
flipped middle finger
to their military might?

Yes, here I am,
dupe of history,
willing to be counted,
to perform on this
stretch of white dust,
my walk of shame
for Cyril Radcliffe.

Poor Cyril:
he grew to rue
the line he drew.

Poor Cyril:
refuser of the money,
burner of the records.

Poor Cyril:
his feet never
touched this ground.

1998

What is my quarrel
with Wagah border?

If I demand intricate lines
woven by radiant dancers
and garlanded singers, Hind,
isn't it merely the welcome
assured to all the granddaughters
of your granddaughters
in your legends
of queens and goddesses?

Wasn't it your vow, Sindh,
chanted over and over
at the birth
of my grandmother's
grandmothers
that the doors of their parents
would never be shut to them?

Do not tell me
how the soldiers
marked their paces
in the white dust
and agreed
to split the difference,
with what ceremony,
to what cadence.

Who I am, even how to walk:
watching them, I no longer know.

I could become Hamlet here,
sulking, disgusted,
scanning this horizon, seeing
no disruption in the skies
that these fences and gates
should divide the earth;
that twenty thousand men
should go to their graves
over a stubbed toe of geography.

I am not the prince
who commanded this dumb-show
of soldiers pumping their knees
and jerking their necks
towards the enemy
with their faces set in glares.

Why did I leave
Wagah border?

To be importuned by its ghosts
and mark my path forever
from where they fell?

In truth its ghosts are too courteous,
their summons came with such reluctance,
that even at the mention of justice –
their dignity will not be offended
with ideas of vengeance –
their pain only deepened into silence.

Is anything left for me
at Wagah border?
I would have learned
well enough without it
from the Sindh of it
and the Hind of it

that when you are about to arrive
and when you are about to depart
that the ones left behind to await you
will gather all their gifts for your safe arrival
and all their strength your safe return
and sweep the steps
and give you apples
and carry your camera
and hold your hand
and forbid you to cry
and stroke your hair
and swallow their sadness
and suppress their joy

that in the glad relief of your arrival
there is already the grief of your departure?

2048

What shall we say
of the stretch of white dust
that was called Wagah border?
People to the Sindh of it
and people to the Hind of it
were pushed from their homes
towards the idea of a line,
forced with fire and knives.

How did we undo Wagah border?
We strove to carry both sides of it
in our minds, as if it were not there.
We spoke aloud the names
of all who died not reaching it.

The soldiers' protests slowly faded
as they left to repair other roads
so girls could ride bicycles to libraries
and boys would not be late for music class.

We undid Wagah border step by step,
smuggling the names
of all who died not reaching it,
through its single point of entry,

carrying them carefully
to streets they fled in pain.
We spoke them aloud,
our defiant act of safe return.

WAGAH BORDER II

1998

Smiling brilliantly
as he stamps my passport
with permission to enter,
what the customs official
at Amritsar wants to know
is have I brought any poems,
and will I recite some for him?

I hear my stunned voice say
that my notebook is strapped
in the overstuffed backpack.
His wild eyebrows
actually widen,
as if I have broken a promise
I had made to him personally
last year or twenty years ago.

Recovering, he asks,
do I know Khwaja Ghulam Farid?
He and his colleague sing together,
Har surat vich aave yaar.

A card of delicate pink and eggshell
arrives in my mailbox months later,
expressing best wishes for the new year.

Your poems,
he writes in blue ink.
Don't forget to send me your poems.

RETURN (FAHMIDA BEGAM)

1

Disappointment turned her face
just once towards mine:
the day I returned from school
with my proud head
wrapped in black cotton,
she shook hers, saying,

"You are young. Why have you put on
that old woman's clothing?"

2

If the muse goes silent,
it is not she who forgets.
She keeps a vigil
charged with purpose.

The poet must startle awake
to the evidence silted up
in all the rooms of her life,

the bare sediment of facts
she has failed to shake loose
from the detritus
of slowly shed time –

3

How brightly Fahmida Begam talked
to her daughters and their daughters
of a hundred other things
could be the true measure
of the depth of her silence.

On her first visit to Canada,
for the marriage of my aunt,
she held my seven-year-old face in her hands,
and declared my ears must be pierced.

She would take me to have this done herself.
Tears filled my eyes in the instant of pain;
I blinked and smiled fiercely, adoring her.

That night my earlobes gleamed
with pure gold, first granddaughter's due.

4

In what coin
must the mother of six daughters
pay out the social currency
that will reward her late days
with richest memory?

Did her feminine effusions
for this engagement or that pregnancy
never betray the slightest boredom,
a restless wish for elsewhere?

By the time she became a Canadian,
her daughters would have little of it;
her granddaughters, still less –

How patiently she heard me
the winter night I returned
eager to repeat in Urdu
the way I'd closed a speech
at a Muslim student gathering –

"Yes, I am a feminist.
Get used to it, brothers!"

I paused, avid for her praise,
which never came.

"Have you brought the video
of my son's wedding reception in Australia,
which I have waited eight weeks to see?"
she asked, with devastating composure.
"Perhaps you could allow me to watch it now."

5

What is the brittleness
of the bride's first return?

Layers of silence,
thinning and hardening,
are about to break.

In Kashmir old songs
of welcome and devotion
would await her;
the delicacies laid out
upon the finest cloth.

But all their Canadian years of rising early
to clear snow off their thoughts
have almost emptied her women of music.

Oh, in absent-minded lulls,
in voices like bright threads
straying loose from long veils
you might hear a phrase or two
sung while running cold water
over a bowl of rice at the sink.

You hear it there:
how the sound of rice
sieved through cold water
remains itself a song of Kashmir,
and the cue for its women to sing.

The bride resumes her place
in her mother's kitchen,
lifting out familiar stacks of plates,
joking indignantly with the cousin
who annexed her favourite mug
after the wedding.

Everyone knows but no one has words
for what has remained unspoken,
what the bride can no more deny,
that her skin and limbs and hair

have warmed to waking,
to their glowing destiny,
in the arms of the chosen,
the fortunate, fortunate groom.

Yet Fahmida Begam
has heard the ardent words
spoken by the groom himself.

Her poised head turns
with a girl's quick eagerness,
to ask her first granddaughter,

"Tell me again.
Does he tell you that he loves you?
Does he say that you are beautiful?"

In her grandmother's voice
the bride hears a torrent let loose:
she imagines centuries of women's voices
as glacial meltwater in spring,
the rush of laughing first confidences
a wedding finally permits.

"Tell me again,
Does he tell you that he loves you?
Does he say that you are beautiful?"

That the language of romance
should be addressed to the bride
does not strike delight
to the very inmost heart
of Fahmida Begam for nothing.

In the telling, the words
become the silver and the linen,
the celebratory table
laid between them.

6

When her short-term memory
began to desert Fahmida Begam
she instructed her daughter
to write pieces of her family history:
the names of her father, mother, and aunts;

that her grandfather,
a secretary in the royal Kashmiri court,
wrote poems limned with sadness
for sons who had died in infancy.

7

What Fahmida Begam
said to us
again and again
in the weeks
before her death:

"I want to go home,
I want to go home.
My parents
will be so happy to see me."

8

You could fault me for delay,
for the way I circle her silence,
reluctant to force it open –

But you never lost her to it;
never watched, helpless,
all the long winters
silence overtook her days;

until you gave in, defeated
by her refusal to speak
when my grandfather died,

when what we most wanted
were detailed, dreamy tellings
of the Kashmir they had, together, made ours;
that Kashmir, where we could never return.

You could fault me for delay,
say I prolong her silence
with incremental unravelling,
and you would be right –

But I would tell you as plaintively
how the most vital facts can slip loose
from the vaguest meandering digression;
that our most startling stories are never told
in the chummy, perfect firelight
for cracked walnuts and peeled tangerines;

but at the precarious edge of narrative, nearly too late,
when at least two aunts have gone yawning off to sleep,
and a cousin stands in the cold front hall
one arm already through a puffy sleeve,
insisting they have to leave
before snow falls again;
in our most startling stories,
snow is nearly always about to fall again.

9

The contents of a letter
written early in 1948
by a Jammu doctor
to Fahmida Begam in Srinagar

have been told and retold
by parents to children, in fragments;
moments saved from disconnect,
resentment, wishing to be elsewhere;
moments spanning decades
on different continents.

Of every merciless act
the doctor witnessed in Jammu
no news reached Kashmir
until she opened its pages.

We know she gathered her strength
to return to the house of her parents,
to scream and weep her rage and loss
before the abashed usurpers;
that it would take ten years
to file the claim and fight the case
that would restore it to her name;
that her younger brother and sisters
who fled to Lahore would write
to tell her they had survived.

But from her first reading of the brutal facts,
can she really have lifted up her head
to another tranquil winter morning
in the paradise of kings?

She was carrying the girl
who, twenty-two years later,
would become my mother.

Could Himalayan steadfastness
brace any woman
after such a body blow?

I hate most
to think of her increasing worry
during those two months
before the letter's arrival;

the longest time that had ever elapsed,
without word from her parents in Jammu
for the teenager, the respected married lady,
Fahmida Begam in Srinagar –

Srinagar, epicentre of her silence,
city of our origin, our loss upon loss.

10

"But tell me again," said Fahmida Begam
on each of my successive returns,
"Does he tell you that he loves you?
Does he say that you are beautiful?"

11

What is the tripwire ringing the alarm?

We prepared elegant tables in her style,
remembering our Kashmiri summers,
arranging the cups for the four o'clock ritual
through all her Canadian winters.

If too little poured out among us
of laughter and frankness,
still we warmed our chilled hands
around the mugs and called it enough,

knowing the feather-light pastry
and the delicate talk that bites at the edges
of the safely feminine, the merely permissible
sustains no woman for her true work;

that no woman can make a life
from how she is seen
in the eyes of anyone else;
that she must speak
with clarity and force
of the world she sees.

12

The summer night of my last return,
she waited with subdued greeting –

I sat down at her table
in confusion and pain
I could speak of to no one.

Could she see from my face
that same door had closed
which had long ago
been shut upon her own?

That I was at risk
of lapsing into the silence
that has so often appeared
to so many of my women
as the work they were cut out for?

Fahmida Begam
asked me no questions
but held up a hand
commanding, listen –

Then words poured from her
with clarity and force,

poems in Urdu and poems in English,
poems of Hali and poems of Iqbal,
poems she had memorized as a girl,
poems she had recited to her parents,
poems my mother was astounded to hear,
poems she would recite every day
until she left us,

let my heart even then
not be anguished.

We had arrived, she and I,
at the hour of the true work
and the magnificent return:

pure gold rinsed clean
in a rush of glacial meltwater.

SEVEN STONES FOR JAMARAT

The Devil appeared to Abraham at the stone-heap of Aqabah. Gabriel said to him, "Pelt him!" so Abraham threw seven stones at him …

– AL-AZRAQI
ninth-century historian of Mecca

The stoning of the three Jamarat is in essence the trampling upon the internal tyrant (An Nafs al Amarah) … while stoning the Jamarat, one must focus entirely upon one's self …

– AYATOLLAH AL HAJJ ASH SHEIKH HUSAIN MAZAHERI
Secrets of the Hajj

FIRST STONE:
OKANAGAN CHERRIES

Woman at the bus stop, waiting.
Driver at the wheel, turning.
Smile when their eyes meet; why not?
Such coincidence prompts goodwill

in such a heat blaze, the season's first.
She trusts him, trusts him still;
propensity she won't question,
sees no reason to break from.

Let them go, then,
this short way together,
in the ready post-marital phrase:
amicably enough.

Driver, eyes on the shimmering road;
woman, watching him eat, steadily,
from a sack perched by his knees,
new summer cherries –

She will review this scene later
from a colder season. She will
take full measure of a distance
already travelled; the speed

of an escape, adroitly worked;
how shrewd the calculation
of a price long since extracted from her,
even for this roadside courtesy;

that her unbroken trust
was the crux of the problem;
her *seeing no reason* a luxury
he could no longer forgive.

Today she only sees the splendid reds –
his private feast. One cherry, after another,
after another, held warm in his mouth,
savoured for a second – then – each stone

bitten clean and pelted out the window.
Each tiny bloodied inconsequential ping –
and why does she laugh? and what is the joke?
– clear as it hits the spinning rims.

Vancouver, 2011

SECOND STONE:
PARENTAL EXHORTATION

The most dangerous ritual in all of Islam –
my father could tell you –
stoning the Jamarat pillars.

How eagerly he warmed to the subject.
Thrice a Hajji, twice he had walked
the two-tiered Jamarat bridge; infamous site

of panic, trampling, and once, fatal collapse.
We would survive the risk, he urged us,
if we embraced it, kept cool heads,
following his example. Pick an hour

after sunset, and climb the bridge
to the second level, moving always towards the exit,
to stone the devils only with escape in sight,
to walk out empty-handed, scot-free –

our Hajj complete. He hoped we would go, and soon,
like other young marrieds; give up our comforts,
test our mettle in the hard sun
and crush of pilgrimage.

We smiled, complicit; guiltily able
neither to assent nor refuse; startled
by such particular insistence, at first greeting,
on the fine points of arcane ritual.

An awkward topic. We abandoned it.
No small talk plumbs Hajj anyway –

Which self would we reject?
Won't some inner demons give our sharpest aim the slip?
Who wants to think about that –?
Sighed rejoinder to all my gloomy questions.

Twelve years later,
you can't throw cherry pits
out the car window fast enough. I think it's hilarious!

Too irreverent for white pilgrim cloth –
your fiction would hold,
spin out longer than any pentitent's fabric –
then unravel in about ten minutes –
in short, we never made it to Mecca –

yet how exactly, after all, you followed his advice.
Pelting your stones from the safe cusp of flight.

Hamilton, 1999

THIRD STONE:
GRAVEL

Consider Said, pausing at the fence
marking the enemy's retreat.

The stone contains time before rude borders.
The stone outlasts the reign of guns and tanks.

How should Said choose his stone?
From this scarred ground, so much
might leap into the palm of his hand –

spilled dust of women's lives
roughly jerked up from four hundred villages,
razor-wired into camps with feminine names –
a pretence of permanence. The children who slept
in the curve of their arms, the blood in their wrists
that pulsed with steady life through the night,
eighteen Septembers ago, until their murders
shook awake the morning –

(Broken, the soldiers admit it now;
their eyes should never have seen
such bright spurts.)

He could choose a stone for mourned Eqbal –

Eqbal, who in boyhood walked for weeks
to another rude border –
in another pilgrimage –
lamentably, quite as Muslim –
the voluntary exile his mother –
from their home in Bihar –
steadfastly refused –

Both friends would have felt it –

how the grief and the work, carried for decades,
can lighten into a moment's quick impulse –
how the heavy planet
of all Said remembers
even the death
that shadows his blood –
can turn weightless
in the hand, vaulted
into lovely triumph –

See its arc through the dusty Lebanon sky!

How the scandalized press
squawks and frets –

How the struck metal –
delightful counterpoint –
chimes!

Liberated South Lebanon, 2000

FOURTH STONE:
NAZARENE PEBBLE

Do I only imagine it? How vengeful
I have become? I am seized
by the will to strike. I could summon
such accusations to circle you now,

a crowd not even Christ would disperse.
Mine would be the first stone by right.
And if its sharp velocity worried him;

if the revered hand, worker of miracles, moved
for your sake, to restrain my elbow? Mine
would be far from the first Muslim poem
Christ has ever appeared in; and if

Muslim imagination has only ever thrived
on borrowed prophets and brazen re-inscribings,
so graciously here would Muslim justice
give way to Christian charity:

You throw like a girl, I imagine,
gently, he'd chide. *Aim high and inside.*
Put your back into it. Here,
give me that stone, I'll show you.

First-century Palestine

FIFTH STONE:
JAMARAT BRIDGE RECONSTRUCTION

Ha! Even against my will, admiration spills
at the reconstruction's massive scale –
not beautiful but austere; ugly in fact, squat heft
of ramps and arcades densifying, yet diffusing,

aerating, coaxing, and cohering through and through
five twelve-metre stories, streams of walkers in white;
their targets, hidden now from aerial view
shelter, too, under sun-deflecting white canopies.

Gone: the pointed pillars of hand-cobbled stone,
by which pilgrims could imagine retracing the steps
of a prophet retracing the sun-beaten steps of a prophet;
the ancient markers now replaced by elliptical shells

of steel and smooth concrete, high and expansive
as the mood they are designed
to keep the faithful in; flowing calmly,
no vexing sharp angles, no flustered sudden turns;

their surfaces perfect iconoclasts; open
to all our projections; inevitable
as puritan Sunni orthodoxy; implacable
as Saudi supremacy; though its engineers insist

the structure's a mere frame for the tides of human volition
sweeping over it. A million arms, canted back; a million devils
imagined in a merciless rain of stones; spurned every hour
to give the new bridge its meaning; its astonishing power.

An immense denunciation, a performance tour-de-force –
starring everybody. So intrigued, so almost do I wish
I could take my place among them, gather my seven stones,
take my chance, take aim! And yet, once I stepped

before the pristine ellipses, my hands resolute, my sights turned inward,
would the devils I repelled not flee to better vantage,
in the new towers gilding Mecca, the gaudy *nafs al amara*
the Keepers of the Haramain keep building?

If I pelted even seven hundred times seven stones?

Mecca, 2007

SIXTH STONE: INTERRUPTION OF A PRESS CONFERENCE

Yes, the shoes he threw
fell wide of their mark –
well the thief invader ducked –
& yes, the guards
closed in swiftly
to drag him to prison
with kicks & blows.

But the air drawn
into the lungs
of Muntadhar al-Zaidi
that long minute ago –
exhaled in a roar –

"This is a farewell kiss
from the Iraqi people,
you dog! This is
for the widows
& orphans
& all those killed in Iraq –"

that shout still rises –
& when the thief invader
has been dust for a century,
that shout will shake the outer planets.

Occupied Baghdad, 2008

SEVENTH STONE: PYREX PLATE

To seize the power of the ancient gesture,
you know a woman must fill it with her own fierce meanings.

Begum Sikandar of Bhopal writes in 1864 of her journey to Mecca
by ship and splendid camel train; of courtly manners nearly lost in translation
between royal houses of Hind and the Hijaz; demands on her generosity so brazen;
outright thefts so frequent, she can only circle the Kaaba in disguise,

under armed Turkish guard; she spares no ink on the arcane rituals.
Lady Evelyn Cobbold of Suffolk, in 1933, gathers seven stones at Mina
right enough, but gets so fussed trying to wake an elderly companion
she forgets to tell the crucial facts: how the pillars looked

when she stood among the thousands that night; if emotion shook
her voice or her elbow; if she pelted her devils with Abraham's own moral might –
(did the Earl of Dunmore's daughter face devils?) Damn it, has no woman
left record, in praise of hurling's righteous outrage, pelting's vicious joy?

A single line by Alice Munro rises from schoolgirl memory; then
its entire poison-laced domestic scene.
The woman cleans the kitchen while her husband berates her –
words to scrape so raw the shared skin of years

I might have taken warning, sickened even at sixteen –
vowed never to leave Ontario. You know
Munro's west coast marriages never end well.
He was still talking as I threw the Pyrex plate at his head.

Pure rage in perfect recall. Pocketed, cool and round, to finish my Jamarat.
(Lemon pie rebounds off the fridge and hits the husband
in the face.) I seize the ancient gesture, weighted
with my fierce gleanings. I never write a verse now but I hurl it.

Fictional Vancouver, 1982

I didn't believe in it for a moment
but I gulped down the wine of my own voice.
And then I wrestled with the darkness inside me,
knocked it down, clawed it, ripped it to shreds.

– LAL DED
fourteenth-century Kashmiri mystic

ART HISTORY

1995

From the snowy street
you move towards her on first sight,
take the table beside the wall
where the framed print hangs;
sling your schoolbooks across,
and drop into the chair;
surprised and pleased
that the artist could know
the feeling of how eyes go hollow
long under electric lights after dark.

There's more to the lady of Automat
than any agreeable magazine face;
hers is a complicated intrigue
you think you recognize as adult,
and return to admire often –

She has slipped off the confines
of merely being seen
and entered the realm of seeing;
despite the chill you imagine
pressed huge against the window;
her thoughts so absorbing
as to interrupt the pulling off
or putting on of the other glove

her inward gaze the still centre
the painting's subtle music radiates from
in yellow and shining brass effusions.

Through her abstracted face you can only look
into yourself, the dignity of her solitude
bracing yours; your resolution
to wring good work from the late hour.

2010

He turns back the page
to reveal her again,
your lady of Automat,
her stilled figure
above the printed grid
of your fortieth November,

a last proprietary act
before quitting the room
by the one who chose the calendar.
As if sunlit reproductions
of Hopper's mid-century
made the ideal timer
by which a marriage
could wind down.

"You're an artist,"
the shrugged pronouncement
offered up as a reason to leave,
a reason you'll whisper again
under your breath, in self-mockery.

How neatly the lady of Automat
brackets your singlehood's stop and start.
Would the warm affinity
you confessed for her
early in your romance
have been better
kept to yourself?

You never guessed
you could become a fleeting face
reflected in plate glass; never thought

your art history could be revived
(the dignity of her solitude
bracing yours) with timing
so vindictive, so exquisite.

APRIL IS WHEN I MOST HATE VANCOUVER

To the sudden brightening
of gilded limbs fatly festooned

some ancestral being must have blinked awake
and, at the edge of sickness, swooned

with the desire to be young again.
To spin the sugar, and colour it like that

some hungry merchant must have dreamed
of selling clouds suffused with evening light

in sticky miniature, a twenty-five cent fantasia
melting to sweet grit in the teeth.

But here some bitterer ephemera
fills my mouth. Think of the vital sap

sucked up the riven green-furred trunk,
urging the buds, *effloresce*

as the tough root's stealth campaign for longevity
in a colour Germaine Greer wants outlawed

for soothing girls and women with the lie, fate's roseate –
warm as lips tracing a persuasive

line of flattery down your neck, past the crook of your arm;
swearing to your fingertips that for beauty

you'll never go hungry again; that's rent money
in bloom; pay no attention to the storm

that strips the branches, swirls and flutters
the blushing tender, forces the wedding

in scurrilous haste, to hailstones. Glory
hardly realized; glory already squandered,

pulped into ruin, into every cracked grey line
of the city you keep waking up from

as nightmare, or party you're always late to,
arriving always fearful

the musicians have left the floor
to the sweeper's broom's silence;

the wantable stranger's already turned away,
shoulders hunched, massive, snow-dusted,

eyes only for the ocean,
while you stare, stupid, famished,

believing in cherries, until not one faint scent
umbrellas the cloudburst upon your head.

BLUE GLASS TULIPS

Our petals array themselves
as dusk overtakes afternoon
in early winter.

At the threshold that guards
the hidden from the visible self,
we preside over the tricky hour
of your increasing gloom

when neither the coat buttoned close,
nor the scarf pulled up to your chin,
nor the sleeves drawn to your wrists,
can stop the horizon from closing in.

Christmas is coming;
relentless time-turner,
venerable Christmas;
measure of belonging,
fought and resented
and loved since girlhood,
your long-gone girlhood,
with every certainty fled
except Christmas is coming
and you're going to be alone –

You're about to go under
saying not a word to anyone;
to pull self-denial over your head
like a civic duty –

We won't let you.
We are the blue glass tulips.

In a dream you will step between
the trench-coated shoulders
of other women we've stopped
in their reluctant homeward tracks.

Look at us. Forget everything
you thought you knew
about the imperatives of melancholy.

Forget Miss Brill,
rushing home past the bakery
with her soul averted.

Forget Holly Golightly,
avoiding her own reflection
in the raw eye of morning.

Ignore the twenty-nine diamonds
clasped around the wrist
of Madame Augelier –

but how frantically she searches all of Paris
for another wild glimpse of her childhood –
think of that –

think of your mother,
lingering after work
at Eaton's window,
coming home to you
with gifts of books and gloves.

We are the blue glass tulips.
In our iridescence,
we see your faces soften.

You try to reason yourself
out of your longing for us –

We tell you reason's a coward,
reason's a bully; we can name
the dollar figure reason sold out for

when you still believed
an orderly God
would arrange to perfection
all the affairs of your heart.

Leave your heart to us.
Delft could shatter for our sake;
the South China Sea
could lose its thirst for aquamarine.

Our petals were turned in fire,
bowled open by human breath.

As low flames, cupped,
we heat in turn the subtle engine
of your looks, the controlled exhale
of your admiration.

What you love in us is the paradox
of movement held fast in glass.

Our petals repeat the undulation
you could not see as beautiful
when your breath moved your body
in the same ecstatic line.

Now you see;
pull your coat tight
about the unyielding
substance of your isolation,
less tangible than cold air,
hard as your boots
hitting hard concrete;
Now you see.

We'll visit you
at waking's edge,
when longing
yaws loudest
in the little bones of your ears.

Go on, turn us this way and that
in the searchlight of your memory.

GRIEF WAKING

In a morning like a drink of cool water
I crave, on waking, the sun-warmed river.

To warm my blood in the current,
release my neck and arms

from grip of wordless dolour.
To dislodge from my throat

the thorns *left alone*
caught there.

To feel the weight of my skull
tipped back, my dark matter set afloat.

To release from the muscles of my eyes
their practised calibrations

of tightening every day
to the shape of your face;

and the memory of your face,
void of any sign

that any face could soften,
beholding mine.

A river after a fire, after a death
that shakes a city.

A river after my anger
as iron hardens after fire,

slow-heating; slower to cool.
A river after my anger,

as banked coals beneath the ash –
a flare, a subsidence, a flare.

A river after my anger,
alien root that coils and burrows,

burrows blind, tears earth,
splits rocks beneath in eternal splitting.

A river after the sun – why not?
Must I submit to grief

in a season of radiance? Won't
my anger rise, throwing off

even the giant that warms my limbs
even now in the healing river?

Hurtled to pinlight at the edge of time,
until it mirrors back nothing

but my anger, freezing, flickering,
burning, waiting, spiteful, bereft?

GRIEF MIRROR

I could not shake it off for months –
Wife – that doll mask peeled loose.

For months I felt its alien weight
pull at the bones and tendons of my face.

Sleep would not ease its clutch,
nor would it be smiled away.

I stared into mirrors with it
to find what I had been before
that I could be again – mine –

I gazed at strangers with it –
as a child who doubts the value
of the cracked, still-bright found object

offers it up, hoping for relief,
for glad recognition; meeting only
cold appraisal, cold as plate glass.

Is this yours? looked my question
Is this yours? the prompt reply
Is this yours? receded in infinity

Anxious faces searched mine for comfort –
that I could be again what I had been before –
until I remembered how to go blind.

TAJWID LESSON

1

To be fearful of making a mistake,
voice humble, heart tremulous with hope:
the proper attitude, according to my teachers,
for beginners in tajwid, the art of Quran recitation.

Once warned of the danger of falling into error –
It would be as if you had changed the meaning –
I dreaded the jaw-ache of mandatory lessons;
increasing fluency gave me no happiness

until the Chapter of The Bright Morning Hours,
ma wadda'aka rabbuka wa ma qala
wal al akhiratu khayrun laka min al ula

"Very good," said the teacher,
brusquely turning to the next twelve-year-old,
while my eyes slid
to the English on the facing page.

My surprise at the compassion and tenderness
in the lines I'd just recited filled my eyes –
not her praise.

I began to think of Arabic vowels
those airborne slash marks, as wings
to lift the heavy earthbound consonants into flight.

2

On our long drives up into the mountains,
and on our drives down the coast
my eyes were drawn again and again to lines of trees,
rooted, solid, black, striving (I thought) for uprightness.

You, at the wheel, would insist on calling my sight
to a patch of nameless sky, to a bird in flight –
you could tell what type by the shape of a wing –
an updrawn breath, a vowel mark,
lifting off from dense huddled forest.

I'd turn to look, nearly always too late –
unless it was a slow ungainly heron –

The days grew more frequent
when I could read your clear marks of withdrawal
but it was as if you had changed their meaning;

the further you retreated, the more you insisted
I could find the way to reach you
if I really wanted; with the proper attitude –

I became confused, fearful of making a mistake;
airborne as a released *ah,* unable to read a consonant
or hovering bird, circling, circling, unable to find
the tree where I could safely land.

And here the metaphor must break.
I have heard female reciters of Quran
go fearlessly into the verses, low-voiced,
virtuoso with passion. Trees fall or endure,
birds take flight and return; of course I returned,

to myself. I came back
standing, striving for uprightness. I see it simply now:
my eyes were drawn to trees for how they stayed –
your eyes were drawn to birds for how they went.

THE WILLOWS

1

That October the willows drew me to them.
Cloaked inside their braided yellow curtains

their shadowed, age-roughed bulk
suggested two bodies, stooped,
inclined towards each other from long habit.

Under clouds, we would say
leaves appear to greater advantage;
in flat grey light, we would say
they seem to glow from within.

But sunlight pressed glitter that day
on the swaying thousands.

I reached for my phone with no thought
but to tell you right away, come see.

But I had left my phone at home.
I took out my pen instead.

I looked at the willows, recalling
how we had agreed,
in the way of married people,
on the importance of close attention,
on silence and reverence; together,

walking and looking
in the way of married people,
we even spoke of effulgence,
transcendence.

Sunlight poured off the slender leaves.
I was elated. I wanted
to make something good
to give to you.

2

I could leave it there,
unfinished poem
found in an old notebook,
consisting of two images:
the willows, calling me to them,
and I, my impulse
to call you thwarted, yielding
to the impulse to write;

with neither experience nor apprehension
of betrayal, believing myself
full of omniscience, up to the eyebrows
with the continuing marvel of our narrative.

How strong the temptation to pull focus,
to show the blinkered vision
on which my delight depended;

to write the scene from your point of view.
Suppose I'd had my phone: carrying

not the lover's voice
to the impatient husband's ear,
but the blithe wife's,
going cluelessly on
about the trees, the light

only the audience sees
the small blade of fact
he keeps hidden
in plain sight.

But I had left my phone at home.
Suppose we flash forward instead,
to a woman released
by the glorious willows,

demanding everything;
all of her love and concentration;
reminding her and warning her
about the cost of resplendence,
the hard solitude of the maker.

MODERN (ABDUL REHMAN)

Master craftsmen
of Samarkand, Iznik, and Esfahan,
how would you look
on the tiles Abdul Rehman made
by hand, from cement,
for honeycombed footpaths
set into the front lawns
of the homes of his daughters?

Would their plain surfaces
cool your eyes,
after all your centuries
of visual prolixity?

Would you read them
as cold weather practicality,
or homage to the modern?

Samarkand, Iznik, and Esfahan,
I declare myself heir
to your discipline of looking:

By the dazzling life of the mind,
you meant the daily hum of your streets;
a complicated music, made visible.

Samarkand, Iznik, and Esfahan,
I'm so enraptured
by your marriages
of corals to turquoises;
cobalts to golds
that for harmony,
can a mere human hand
outstretched to another
ever compare?

Your tulips and saz leaves,
your arcades of tangled geometry,
rebuke, from across four centuries,
that I'm missing the point;

that you hold in your beholder
the anticipation of how,
in what precise lyrical sphere,
to be properly humanly held.

Stay, say the Shah-i-Zindah,
the Shah Mosque, the Sultan Ahmet;
stay, you have arrived
at the centre of your world;
you won't need to flee
anywhere else.

Samarkand, Iznik, and Esfahan,
I see how younger cities
covet your adornments.

Radiant pieces of you
keep turning up in their museums,
to give them size and cover the fear
that wealth might shrink them.

In cinema after cinema,
the century that cast you aside
and let you fall into ruin,

promised us how elegantly
the smoke would curl
in the lamplight of our solitude;

how the streets would urge us on
to our departures and arrivals;
that our happiness would hang
on our ability to go
and keep going.

Samarkand, Iznik, and Esfahan,
for the last twenty years of his life,
Abdul Rehman would bend his back
over the work, in total absorption,
breathing clouds of cement dust
in with his air, to his daughters' despair.

On the low bench
of nailed-together wood,
we saw him select his tools
cut his stencils, mix chips
of marble or quartz
into the cement,
make pots and tables
to adorn the gardens
of his daughters
and the friends of his daughters.

We grapple with his absence
the way we honoured his instruction
to bury him without the janaza:

reading the single linear arabesque
he often printed around the rims
in grey or blue or pink or black,

as echo of the hexameters and medallions
your painters and carvers repeated
as countlessly as the telling of beads
by worshippers in acute need of peace.

In Srinagar his street lamps ring the Dal,
his fountains and park benches invite passersby
to stay, defy curfew, give life
to myths of kings: *Only Kashmir –*

In truth he wanted out, chafed against
the war games and quagmire
for which India and Pakistan
abandoned the onyx and carnelian
of their real names.

In truth, he wanted to see New York.

Samarkand, Iznik, and Esfahan,
how did airport corridors
that repeat and repeat
become the template
for our modern street?

You are here, the cities assure us,
as long as your *here*
agrees with our slippery *anywhere*;
glossing the snags and fault lines

that messy human sentiment
constantly strives to cling to –
keeps moving, keeps pushing along.

Yet I have paced the concrete walks
for hours on my bitterest days;
and found relief nowhere
but in their unbroken
placelessness,

unknowing whether the swept slate
of their *la ilaha*
paves over or clears the way
for the blaze of your *illallah*.

THE LAST SEVEN MINUTES OF *L'ECLISSE*

Am I really her,
woman still blinking awake
at the wide cold crosswalk,
all concrete and tar, all wind rush
and worried truck rumble;

one hand of habitual caution
on the shoulder of the son
she's taking to school, not prayers,
on the morning of Eid ul Adha?

Who am I, if no one else here
knows what name I call today,
how to greet me with it?

Why doesn't someone disapprove,
scold me for standing here,
not in cosseted, hushed worship;
demand why my thoughts aren't filled
with recitations of praise
but the last sad, strange
seven minutes of *L'Eclisse*?

Have I succumbed
to the unbreakable anonymity
the streets planned for me?

No one remembers the Eid
we took over a coffee house,
then spilled into the street,
improbably sharp-dressed
for a Wednesday morning,
glad for the trick of time
that let us stretch out

our holiday mood
for several city blocks;
how our conversation
bloomed and ebbed
earnest and serious,
quoting Dr. Shariati
famously asking,
What is your Ishmael?
– then broke up in hilarity.

No one sees how,
with every stranger who passes
intent on the ordinary day,
I become even stranger to myself;

remembering those seven minutes
of growing certainty
that Monica Vitti and Alain Delon
would refuse to meet again
at the crossroads;

that after all their embrace
was only a self-conscious pantomime
of other people's embraces; they knew
even beauty would not shield them
from a future of divided holidays;
even their fights
about children and money
would look unconvincing
as the streetlights of Rome
blinked on and off.

Truck rumble halts,
we cross the wide walk,
bewilderment pumping
with every step,
in steady doses
up my neck,
down my spine.

I tell myself again
how Mecca was founded
in the steps of a woman
frantically running seven times
between two desert hills
named for the daughters of other women,
on a hot day, in search of water.

FOR THOSE WHO DWELL IN NORTH-FACING APARTMENTS

To content oneself in a small space –
The shrinking eco-footprint's might?
Or poet's true domestic art? My shadow-lines
loom tall in refracted light.

A high window reflects a thin crescent –
if you crane your neck to the right –
No horizon, just the puddle-slicked alley –
We time Maghrib by refracted light.

Of greatness, what measure square footage?
We'd pierce clouds at needle-point heights.
Trading up: the realtor swears we deserve it!
We hone our aspirations in refracted light.

Sometimes, the way he looks at her –
Could be longing. Could be pure spite.
Ambivalent boys play a really cool game
called Maybe, in refracted light.

And yes, her heart, when he looks at her –
But modesty rules, all right.
No moth ever burned its wings at the glass
that tempered refracted light.

If the truth blinds in the daytime
And its absence terrifies by night –
What I want turns restless in shade upon shade –
Meet me halfway in refracted light.

Some quarrels only deepen the connection –
Some grand gestures protract the fight.
And ah, my foes and oh, my friends
Sometimes blur in refracted light.

MARRIED TO ENGLISH
(LINES COMPOSED AT BROCKTON OVAL)

From your moss-pelted north face
and your pearled grey Junes, English,

I learn to love your sunny hesitations better
than if I were driven to seek the shade

from gorgeous Urdu's melting afternoons.
English, how perfectly wedded I am to you.

Here's the ring paved smooth: my dark fidelity.
Here's turf enough to pledge my troth,

and men to sport white for passion,
for the pageant of giving me away.

And they give me away, English,
in every one of your riot-scorched capitals

with raised toasts for shaken fists,
with tea at halftime, and *how lovely to see you today*

by evening post. You do the thing
decently, English. Your sixes and factory bricks

make little rooms for girls like the girl I was,
your child bride, to hide in; your attics and alcoves

just suit the neat points of our elbows.
Our eyes mirror the shine

off your rows of gilt-stamped spines,
and apples gleam in your dim cellars.

So we munch, knees tucked,
content as orphans

grown already forgetful
of the names of our parents' killers.

Pitiless English, what have I become?
My eyes turn in the gloaming,

take delight from the patterned edge
of lichen bound tightly to stone.

At home in the Himalayas my sisters laugh –
the soldiers nail CLOSED MILITARY ZONE

into the flourishing poplars
with your unconquerable precision.

Will you do me the honour, English? Will you permit
this hand to claim the cool sleeve of your pen?

From your daggers and turnkeys I've learned
possessiveness – here my grip tightens – to say,

I'm yours, I'm yours – your humble servant,
your strictest praetor; the wrathful scourge

of your ill-users and callow prattlers –
yours devotedly, English, yours till death.

It's true, I whisper tender Arabic curses
over lies you swore were sterling; I console myself

with half-remembered Farsi endearments.
You keep aloof from their antique silver

but make a din of clumsy names
for pleasures that silence other tongues –

then I blush for you, English.
You indulge every sequin stitched into chiffon

however patient my mudra-curled fingers,
you know the silk ends crushed and tear-stained;

you like my dark lashes so doubled. You hold me
rapt every night; every night you exult, you fool,

believing, with your tongue in my mouth,
I can never say I'm leaving.

NOTES ON SOURCES

It has been centuries since my friend was my guest,
when with language alone, we have lit candles through the night.
– MIRZA GHALIB

|| Urdu couplets in the Nastaliq script, like pairs of open arms, appear throughout every chapter of Sara Suleri Goodyear's memoir and elegy to her father, *Boys Will Be Boys: A Daughter's Elegy* (University of Chicago Press, 2003).

The enigmatic brevity of the *shairi* – now Ghalib's, now Iqbal's – pulled me into their world. Suleri's prose style swept aside several conceptual hurdles I hadn't realized I'd been struggling to overcome, combining multilingual insouciance with smacks of humour and darkness. Having grown up with a similar mix (my mother and aunts kept Kashmiri for the expression of their own private thoughts; my father's family spoke mainly Punjabi; we children were expected to speak Urdu), I could see no excuse for the wretched monolingual state into which I had lately fallen. I began to think and write in a way that would have struck me as impossible ten years earlier; now, like teaching myself to read Nastaliq, it had become merely necessary.

|| In *I, Lalla: The Poems of Lal Ded,* Indian translator and critic Ranjit Hoskote describes the poet who renounced her home and marriage to become a devotee of Shiva at age twenty-six as a "liminal figure," a "woman who made heterodox choices," and "a wanderer who had deliberately de-classed herself." "Called *vakhs,* Lalla's poems are among the earliest-known manifestations of Kashmiri literature," he writes. "The Persian terms that appear in the Lal Ded corpus indicate a rendering of her ideas in Sufi phraseology. Such acts of translation would follow naturally in an environment where philosophies were in dialogue" (New Delhi: Penguin India, 2011), ix*ff.*

|| Somehow the story of Lal Ded wandering unconcernedly naked around Kashmir, singing and meditating, until the moment she saw Shah Hamadan, exclaiming "I have seen a man!" and leaping into a fiery oven, even made it into my puritan Sunni (via Protestant work-ethic) upbringing, ecumenical *bhai-bhai* inferences and all. Alluding to the moment in the legend when she emerged, unharmed and regally clothed, to greet

the Sufi sheikh as a respected equal, in his poem, "I Dream I Am the Only Passenger on Flight 423 to Srinagar," Agha Shahid Ali asks, "Was it thus / that Lal Ded – robed in the brilliant green / of Paradise – rose from her ashes, fabulous // with *My body blazed*? Could she have then foreseen / the tongue survive its borrowed alphabets?" (*The Country without a Post Office: Poems* [New York: W.W. Norton, 1997], 33).

|| Art historians and design mavens already know how Owen Jones, nineteenth-century English architect and designer, drew profound inspiration from Islamic art ("so much unity of design, so much skill and judgment in its application, with so much of elegance and refinement"). In his 1856 magnum opus *The Grammar of Ornament*, Jones singles out for attention the "gorgeous contributions" of India:

From the highest work of embroidery, or most elaborate work of the loom, to the constructing and decorating of a child's toy – there is always the same care for the general form. The same division and subdivision of their general lines, which forms the charms of Moresque ornament, is equally to be found here; the difference which creates the style is not one of principle, but of individual expression. In the Indian style ornaments are somewhat more flowing and have, doubtless, been more subjected to direct Persian influence. The Indian collection at South Kensington Museum should be visited and studied by all in any way connected with the production of woven fabrics. In this collection will be found the most brilliant colours perfectly harmonized. (*The Grammar of Ornament*, [reprinted London: Herbert Press, 2010], 241*ff*).

|| *The Death of the Urdu Script* is the title of a wonderful essay, published online at *Medium* by Ali Eteraz on October 7, 2013, about the highly technical yet aesthetic dilemma of coding an Urdu typeface for cellphones and the Internet. Eteraz's plaintive description of Naskh as "this pretender font" sparked my imagination and sent me back to reading about the history of calligraphy. What if Nastaliq were a woman?

|| The Hajj stories of Sikandar, Begum of Bhopal, Lady Evelyn Cobbold of Dunmore, and many other humbler characters, can be found in *One Thousand Roads to Mecca: Ten Centuries of Travelers Writing about the Muslim Pilgrimage*, edited by Michael Wolfe (New York: Grove Press, 1997).

ACKNOWLEDGEMENTS / REMERCIEMENTS

Wayde Compton affirmed the importance of the page from the beginning. Renee Saklikar and SFU Lunch Poems brought me into one of the city's best reading rooms; George Fetherling loaned much kind support and an authoritative library; Garry Thomas Morse sought out my work after singing opera in the Teck Gallery (I mean, who does that?) and brought me on board at Talonbooks; publisher Kevin Williams, editor Gregory Gibson, designer Les Smith, copyeditors Rolf Maurer and Chloë Filson, and managing editor Ann-Marie Metten gave *Cosmophilia* their meticulous attention and far-seeing generosity; Phinder Dulai embraced the spirit of the thing with warmth and sensitive editorial discernment. (He made it *fun.*)

Shukriyah to The Writers Studio Reading Series, to Michael Callahan at *Exile Literary Quarterly*, and to Barbara Carter at *The New Quarterly*.

Marguerite Pigeon championed both "Wagah Border" and the multilingual condition. Sean Cranbury welcomed me and Amir Khusro to the Real Vancouver Writers' Series and Books on the Radio. Anakana Schofield dispensed tea and upright solidarity at her kitchen table. Heather Menzies has provided thoughtful encouragement alongside lovely hospitality for many years.

Mohja Kahf, azizatu nafsiha, wrote me a scream-worthy letter about poetry more than twenty years ago; Mahwash Shoaib thinks Shahid would have approved; Seemi Ghazi, reciprocal reciter of ghazals in unforeseen hospital rooms, keeps the keys to Arabic on the ancestral lands of the Musqueam people; Kirby Huminuik urged me to throw the stones as hard as I could. Hanane Benzidane, Kelty Miyoshi McKinnon, Naheed Mustafa, Suzanne Muir, Mariam Jalabi, Krista Riley, Anjum Mir, and Jihad Turk illuminate the windows of this North America. Jahanzeb Hussain, Sumayya Syed, and Fathima Cader graced Vancouver with style and remain companions of literature everywhere they go.

I could a tale unfold of the excellence and unsurpassed kindness of Cecily Rampling. Hashmat Khan consistently elevates family to an active verb in its farthest outposts. Nazli Rehman brought me a coveted dictionary of Urdu poetry from her travels; the peerless Dehlavi Reyhan Chaudhuri sent me a history of Ghalib in a hand-sewn parcel (everyone at the post office swooned and wept); Sabiha Rehman exemplifies the hard solitude of the maker; Seema Rehman and Mujeeb Rehman lighten it with their voices; Farhat Rehman keeps everyone stocked with exactly the right art supplies; together with her parents, she gave me Urdu and Kashmir; with my siblings and cousins, she has aided and abetted, stoked the fire, steeped and infused the dreaming and making of this book.

As soon as it was finished, Aijaz Said Karim cheered, ordered a pizza, and insisted on a fierce game of whip-the-hackysack-across-the-room-at-each-other.

Rahat Kurd was born in Hamilton, Ontario, and lives in Vancouver, British Columbia. Her prose has appeared in *The Walrus*, *Maisonneuve*, and other Canadian magazines. The poem sequence "Seven Stones for Jamarat" was a finalist for the 2014 Gwendolyn MacEwen Poetry Prize. *Cosmophilia* is her first collection of poems.